Exceptional Asians

YO-YO MA

Classical Musician

Therese Shea

E **Enslow Publishing**
101 W. 23rd Street
Suite 240
New York, NY 10011
USA

enslow.com

Words to Know

civilian—A person who is not a member of the military, police, or fire department.

composer—One who creates music.

culture—The beliefs, habits, and traditions of a group of people.

genre—A type of artistic work that has a certain form, style, or subject.

orchestra—A group of musicians who play mainly classical music.

recital—A performance given by a solo musician.

scoliosis—A condition in which the spine is curved.

score—Music that has been composed for a movie, play, or musical.

suite—A set of musical pieces meant to be performed together.

unaccompanied—Playing alone.

Contents

Yo-Yo Ma

CHAPTER 1

Musical Beginnings

Yo-Yo Ma is the most famous cellist in the world and one of the most famous classical musicians. His success comes from more than natural talent or practice. He draws on the music of many **cultures**. From an early age, he was exposed to different musical traditions.

Yo-Yo Ma was born to Chinese parents in Paris, France, on October 7, 1955. His mother was a singer, and his father was a **composer** and music teacher. He introduced music early to Yo-Yo and his sister Yeou-Cheng. Yo-Yo began learning the violin as soon as he learned to walk. By the age of four, he began playing the cello.

Learning to Play

Yo-Yo has said that his father's teaching helped him develop his talent early on. The Ma children sometimes woke as early as 4 a.m. to practice. By age five, Yo-Yo knew three of Johann Sebastian

Yo-Yo, age six, plays his cello while his sister Yeou-Cheng plays the violin.

Yo-Yo Says:

"I do believe that a really nurturing first teacher that makes the child love something is crucial."

Bach's **suites** for **unaccompanied** cello by heart and performed in his first public **recital**.

Yo-Yo and his family moved to New York City when he was seven. He performed with **orchestras** and on TV throughout his childhood. He later attended the famous Juilliard School for performing arts. When Yo-Yo was sixteen years old, he entered Harvard University. He studied many subjects, including science and literature.

CHAPTER 2

A Rocky Start

Yo-Yo graduated from Harvard in 1976, ready to start his music career again. He married Jill Hornor, a violinist, the following year.

At the age of twenty-five, Yo-Yo found out he had **scoliosis**. Because he had to bend over his cello while playing, the condition would only grow worse. He had to have an operation. It was possible that he would never play the cello again.

Though the operation was a success, Yo-Yo wore a body cast for six months while he recovered. It made him realize how much he loved the cello and was lucky to be able to play it.

Yo-Yo and Jill have two children, Nicholas and Emily. Both play music like their parents.

A Successful Musician

Yo-Yo bounced back after his surgery and began an amazing career. He mastered classical pieces for the cello. He performed solo recitals, in small groups, and with entire orchestras.

Yo-Yo plays two instruments: a Montagnana cello from Venice, Italy, made in 1733 and a 1712 Davidoff Stradivarius. He mostly uses the Montagnana, which is nicknamed "Petunia."

In the 1990s, Yo-Yo began to introduce new twists to old standards. He credits the many cultures in his

Yo-Yo Says:

"Those things you've gone through add to your life experience and therefore your understanding of the music, and there's more depth to your communicating of the music."

Yo-Yo once left his beloved "Petunia," worth $2.5 million, in a taxi. It was safely returned to him, though.

own background—French, Chinese, and American—to his search for connections between musical traditions.

CHAPTER 3

Wide-Ranging Career

Yo-Yo has always been interested in the music of other cultures. A trip to Africa in 1993 opened his mind to new sounds even more. He listened as Bushmen in the Kalahari Desert used instruments of bones, sticks, and cans to create music. He watched as others responded. In the years that followed, Yo-Yo continued to study other musical traditions and share what he learned in an effort to keep their music alive.

Yo-Yo Ma has also performed with singers and musicians of other **genres** such as reggae singer

Bobby McFerrin, jazz trumpeter Chris Botti, and composer and conductor John Williams.

A Famous Face

Yo-Yo Ma was asked to perform music for the 2000 movie *Crouching Tiger, Hidden Dragon*. The movie was a great success, and so was the music. It won an Academy Award for best original **score**. Yo-Yo gained even more fans.

Yo-Yo Says:

"Jazz has been such a force in music, that any musician, including classical composers, have been influenced."

Yo-Yo plays with musician Jon Batiste and his band on *The Late Show With Stephen Colbert.*

Yo-Yo's face has become almost as recognizable as his music. He has appeared on many television shows, including *The Simpsons.* He has brought classical music to young people through his work on *Sesame Street*, *Mister Rogers' Neighborhood*, and the cartoon *Arthur*. In each, he taught about the cello and about different pieces of music.

Yo-Yo enjoys teaching and playing with young people. In 2014, he was given the Fred Rogers Legacy Award for his work with youth.

Yo-Yo plays at the prayer service after the Boston Marathon bombing.

In Good Times and Bad

Yo-Yo Ma has played at the world's most beautiful concert halls. He has performed for eight US presidents, including many kinds of celebrations. He has also been called to provide music in times of tragedy.

Yo-Yo performed at the first anniversary concert for the victims of the September 11, 2001, terrorist attacks as well as a service following the Boston Marathon bombing in 2013. For both, he chose to play Johann Sebastian Bach's Cello Suite No. 5 in C Minor. He said he chose the piece because the rising notes represent the human spirit trying to rise above tragedy.

CHAPTER 4

Cultural Connections

Yo-Yo Ma started the Silkroad organization in 1998. It is named for the ancient trade route that linked Asia and Europe. Goods were traded along the route as well as ideas. Just as Yo-Yo embraces the music and arts of other cultures, Silkroad works to connect artists around the world and expose audiences to the art of many cultures.

Silkroad also supports the Silk Road Ensemble, a group of performers and composers from different

Yo-Yo plays with the Silk Road Ensemble, a group of artists from more than twenty countries.

backgrounds. They both entertain and educate through their performances. Yo-Yo Ma remains Silkroad's artistic director to this day.

The World's Music

Yo-Yo Ma has released ninety albums and won eighteen Grammy Awards. He has meant so much to the music world that he was awarded the National Medal of Arts in 2001. In 2010, he was given the

Presidential Medal of Freedom, the highest US **civilian** honor.

Yo-Yo is currently serving as a United Nations Messenger of Peace. This is a fitting position for the cellist who believes that music has no boundaries and can build bridges between people of all different cultures.

Yo-Yo Says:

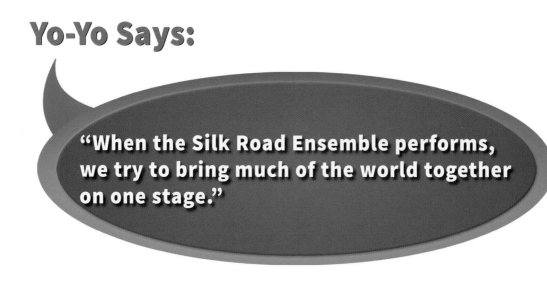

"When the Silk Road Ensemble performs, we try to bring much of the world together on one stage."

Yo-Yo has said he believes music can act as a magnet to draw people together.

Timeline

1955—Yo-Yo Ma is born in Paris, France, on October 7.

1959—Begins playing the cello.

1962—Moves with his family to New York City.

1976—Graduates from Harvard.

1978—Marries Jill Hornor.

1980—Undergoes surgery for scoliosis.

1984—Wins first Grammy Award.

1993—Travels to Africa.

1998—Establishes the Silkroad organization.

2006—Becomes a United Nations Messenger of Peace.

2010—Receives the Presidential Medal of Freedom.

2013—Performs at a service to honor the victims of the Boston Marathon bombing.

2014—Wins the Fred Rogers Legacy Award for his work with children.

Learn More

Books

Ganeri, Anita. *Stringed Instruments*. Mankato, MN: Smart
     Apple Media, 2012.

Hord, Colleen. *A Listen to Classical Music*. Vero Beach, FL:
     Rourke Educational Media, 2014.

Louie, Ai-Ling. *Yo-Yo and Yeou-Cheng Ma: Finding Their Way*.
     Bethesda, MD: Dragoneagle Press, 2012.

McCann, Michelle Roehm. *Boys Who Rocked the World*.
     Hillsboro, OR: Beyond Words, 2012.

Websites

silkroadproject.org
     Learn more about Silkroad, the nonprofit organization
     started by Yo-Yo Ma.

yo-yoma.com
     Read the latest news about Yo-Yo Ma on his official
     website.

npr.org/artists/15995808/yo-yo-ma
     Find links to performances and interviews here.

Index

Published in 2017 by Enslow Publishing, LLC.
101 W. 23rd Street, Suite 240, New York, NY 10011

Library of Congress Cataloging-in-Publication Data
Names: Shea, Therese.
Title: Yo-Yo Ma : classical musician / Therese Shea.
Description: New York : Enslow Publishing, [2017] | Series: Exceptional Asians | Includes bibliographical references and index.
Identifiers: LCCN 2015044485| ISBN 9780766078376 (library bound) | ISBN 9780766078437 (pbk.) | ISBN 9780766078031 (6-pack)
Subjects: LCSH: Ma, Yo-Yo, 1955---Juvenile literature. | Cellists--Biography--Juvenile literature. | Chinese American musicians--Biography--Juvenile literature. | LCGFT: Biographies.
Classification: LCC ML3930.M11 S54 2016 | DDC 787.4092--dc23
LC record available at http://lccn.loc.gov/2015044485

Printed in Malaysia

To Our Readers: We have done our best to make sure all website addresses in this book were active and appropriate when we went to press. However, the author and the publisher have no control over and assume no liability for the material available on those websites or on any websites they may link to. Any comments or suggestions can be sent by e-mail to customerservice@enslow.com.

Photo Credits: Throughout book, ©Toria/Shutterstock.com (blue background); cover, p. 1 Paul Morigi/Getty Images Entertainment/Getty Images; p. 4 Paul Morigi/Getty Images for Ovation; p. 6 Bill Johnson/The Denver Post via Getty Images; p. 9 Andreas Rentz/Getty Images; p. 11 Linda Davidson/The Washington Post via Getty Images; p. 14 Jeffrey R. Staab/CBS via Getty Images; p. 15 Mark Weber/The Commercial Appeal/ZUMA Press; p. 16 JEWEL SAMAD/AFP/Getty Images; p. 19 Hiroyuki Ito/Getty Images; p. 21 Jeff Fusco/Getty Images.